Python Programming

The Crash Course to Learn Programming Python Faster and Remember It Longer. Includes Hands-On Projects and Exercises for Machine Learning, Data Science Analysis, and Artificial Intelligence

Table of Contents

Introduction
Chapter 1: What is Deep Learning and Artificial Intelligence
Chapter 2: A Look at Machine Learning
Chapter 3: An Introduction to Python
Chapter 4: The Scikit-Learn Library
Chapter 5: Creating a Neural Network with Scikit-Learn
Chapter 6: The TensorFlow Library
Chapter 7: K-Nearest Neighbors and K-Means Clustering
Chapter 8: Decision Trees and Random Forests in Machine Learning
Chapter 9: The Linear Classifier and What This Means
Chapter 10: Are Recurrent Neural Networks Different From Neural Networks
Chapter 11: What Else Can I Do with Python Programming and Machine Learning?
Conclusion

Introduction

Congratulations on downloading *Python Programming* and thank you for doing so.

The following chapters will discuss everything that you need to know in order to get started with Python programming. There may be many different options out there that you can choose from when it comes to coding your programs, but none of them can offer you the versatility, and all of the benefits, that you are going to be able to get with Python, and that is exactly what we are going to discuss when we are in this guidebook.

To start this guidebook, we are going to take a look at a few different topics that are ever more increasingly being discussed in relation to Python. We will spend a few chapters looking at artificial intelligence and deep learning, as well as taking in some information about machine learning before starting our own introduction into the Python language and what it is all about.

After this kind of introduction, it is time to start diving into all of the cool things that Python is able to do with machine learning and deep learning, and what better way to do this than taking a look at some of the different libraries of Python that were designed to work with this topic. We will spend some time looking at the Scikit-Learn library, how to create some neural networks with this library, and the TensorFlow library as well.

To finish this guidebook, we are going to spend our time taking a look at a few of the different algorithms that work with machine learning, and how you can use Python to help you write the codes that are needed to make those algorithms work. Some of the best machine learning algorithms that we are going to explore will include the K-Means clustering, K-Nearest Neighbors, Decision Trees, Linear Classifiers and more.

Machine learning and artificial intelligence are becoming like big buzzwords in the industry, and many people are interested in learning how to use them for their own needs and their own kind of programming. While this is a great thing, many of these same people worry that these topics are going to be too hard to learn and to understand. With the help of the information in this guidebook, you will be able to really work on all of this, even as a beginner, with the help of Python. When you are ready to learn how to do some Python programming, and how it can work with machine learning, deep learning, and artificial intelligence, make sure to check out this guidebook to help you get started!

There are plenty of books on this subject on the market, thanks again for choosing this one! Every effort was made to ensure it is full of as much useful information as possible, please enjoy!

Chapter 1: What is Deep Learning and Artificial Intelligence

There are a lot of different parts that can come with coding and working with computers in our modern world. Many people feel that if they don't know how to do a complicated kind of coding, then they are not going to be able to do any at all. But this is just not true. There are many complex types of programming that you are able to do, and they are easier to complete than you may think. And in tis guidebook, we are going to take some of our time to discuss many of them.

To start out with in this chapter, we are going to take a look at deep learning and artificial intelligence. Both of these are going to be integral parts when we are looking at some of the topics that are in this guidebook, and knowing how to make them work, and what all we are able to do with them can make a difference in our coding and what we are able to do in the process. Some of the things that we need to know concerning deep learning and artificial intelligence will include the following:

What is deep learning

The first topic that we are going to spend some time on in this chapter is going to be deep learning. Deep learning is actually a type of machine learning (we will discuss more about that in the next chapter), that is going to be responsible for training our computer how to perform some of the life tasks that humans do. There are a variety of tasks that could fall into this category, but things like recognizing speech, identifying what is inside a picture, and making predictions can all fit into this idea.

Instead of organizing the data to run through equations that are already defined, deep learning is going to set up some of the basic parameters that you need for the data, and then will train the computer to learn on its own by being able to see the patterns through many different layers of processing.

Let's dive into this a bit more. Deep learning is important here because it is going to be a foundation of AI, or artificial intelligence, and the current interest that we are seeing in this deep learning is due to how it is related to AI. Deep learning and some of the techniques that come with it have been able to improve the ability of machines to describe, detect, recognize, and classify things in a way that was previously thought to only work for humans.

A good example of this is all of the different things that deep learning is already able to do in our world. We can find that many of the algorithms and techniques that work with it are great at describing the content that it is going to look through, at detecting objects, and recognizing the speech patterns of those using it, while recognizing what is inside one of the images that you present to it. There are many pieces of technology that use this, such as fraud detection, facial recognition, and systems like Cortana and Siri to name a few.

There are already a few developments who are working on advancing what we see with deep learning. Some of these are going to include:

1. The improvements that have been done on some of the algorithms have been able to boost up some of the methods that we see with deep learning.
2. There are some newer approaches to deep learning that have ensured that the accuracy of the models is going to stay intact.
3. There are even some neural networks that have new classes that are developed to fit well for some new applications, including the classification of images and the translation of text.
4. There is a ton of information available from companies, much more than was there in the past. This helps us to build up some new neural networks with a lot of deep layers,

including streaming data, physicians notes, investigative transcripts, and even some textual data that you could get from social media.
5. There are also some computational advances of distributed cloud computing and graphics processing units which can give us all of the computing power that is needed in order to make sure the algorithms for deep learning can actually be done.

At the same time that all of that is going on, the human to machine interface that we are used to seeing is changing quite a bit as well. The keyboard and the mouse that were traditionally used are now being replaced with things like natural language, touch, gesture, and swipe. This opens up the field to even more AI and deep learning along the way.

This brings up the question of how deep learning can provide us with a lot of opportunities and applications in the process. A lot of power computationally is going to be needed in order to solve some of the deep learning problems, simply because the nature of iterations in these algorithms. This results in the complexity going up as the layers increase as well. And you also need to be able to handle a ton of data at the same time in order to get the networks trained and ready to go.

The dynamic nature of the methods of deep learning, and their ability to always adapt and improve to some of the changes in the underlying information pattern, will present us with the information and opportunity that we need to introduce a bit more of the dynamic behavior that is needed into the analytics.

In addition, we can add in a lot more of the personalization that customers want when the analytics comes into play with deep learning. Another great opportunity here is to improve the performance and accuracy of applications where the neural network is not brand new, but has been around for a longer period of time. through some better algorithms, and more power to compute, we are able to get the benefit of adding in more depth.

The next thing that we can focus on is some of the different ways that you are able to use deep learning to help your business grow and to create some of the great technology that is needed at the same time. To someone who is not all that familiar with how this technology works, it may seem like deep learning is going to be the research phase for computer science and you won't be able to use it that much. However, it is possible to bring in some deep learning in many practical manners to businesses, and it is possible that you are already using quite a few of them today, and didn't even notice the technology that is there.

Some of the different ways that deep learning is being used today and how we can benefit from it as well will include:

Speech recognition. Pretty much every industry in our world has seen some sort of use when it comes to speech recognition. If you have ever asked a question to a device, including your phone, to get an answer, then you have used this. Other places like Skype, Xbox, Google Now, and more are using this as well. The deep learning part is brought in because it helps the system to be able to not only recognize when someone is talking to it, but also know what the person is saying or asking as well.

Natural language processing is another place where deep learning is going to come into play. Neural networks, which are going to be a big component of deep learning, and that we will discuss in more detail later on, have already been used to process and even analyze some written texts for a long time. A specialization that comes with text mining, this kind of technique can be used in other places to discover the patterns that are found in places like news reports, the notes that a physician writes out for later, the complaints from some customers, and even more.

Deep learning can also come into play to help out with recognizing images. One of the more practical applications of this is with automatic image captioning and description of the scenes that are going on. This could be used in a lot of different contexts. But one of these is going to be an example of law enforcement investigations to identify some of the criminal activities that are present in the thousands of photos that bystanders in a busy area have submitted. This is just one example though. A self-driving care could benefit from this kind of technology when it is able to use its camera in all angles to go in the right direction.

And the fourth application that we can discuss when it comes to deep learning, although not the last, is going to be the recommendation systems. There are a lot of different companies who are using this, but some common examples of how this would work include Netflix and Amazon. The point of this is to check what you may be the most interested in next, based on the behavior that you have done in the past. Deep learning is going to be used in order to enhance some of the recommendations that happen in environments that are more complex, such as music interests or your preferences of clothing, even when they occur across more than one platform.

There is so much that you are able to do with deep learning and the world of this kind of programming is bound to keep growing in the future. Understanding what it is all about and how it can work will make a big difference in the amount of success that you are going to see with it over time as well!

What is artificial intelligence

The next kind of topic that we are going to spend some time on is that of artificial intelligence. This is going to be a kind of area of computer science that is going to emphasize how we can create machines that are intelligent, ones that are able to work and react in a manner that is similar to how humans did. There are a lot of different activities that computers that hold onto the artificial intelligence technology are designed for, and these are going to include things like:

1. Planning
2. Problem solving
3. Learning
4. Speech recognition

One thing that we can remember when we are working with artificial intelligence is that it is a branch of computer science. In this particular branch, we are going to aim to create machines that are intelligent, ones that are able to learn and think on their own. In fact, this has become such a prevalent thing in our world that it is know an essential part of the technology industry and we are going to see it grow and take off more than ever before.

There has been a lot of research done on artificial intelligence, especially with how much it has risen in popularity over the last few years. This kind of research has been focused and turned into something that is more specialized and highly technical like nothing before. The core problems that come with artificial intelligence are going to be that we need to be able to program a computer for a lot of different traits, and to get it to behave and think in a manner that is almost the same, but faster and more efficient, than we see with a human.

This is going to be complicated, and many programmers, both newer and more advanced, are going to wonder how we are supposed to make this happen at all. And is it really something that we are able to focus on and do, or are we just wasting our time with all of this? You will find that artificial intelligence has really started to take the world by storm, not because it is just a neat theory, but because of all the neat things that it is able to do in the process.

Right now, there are a lot of different ways that artificial intelligence can be used. And some of the things that we are already able to train a computer to do with the help of this technology will include the following:

1. The ability to move and manipulate any of the objects that you would like.
2. Planning
3. Problem solving
4. Reasoning
5. Learning
6. Perception
7. Knowledge

One of the core parts that you are going to see with some of this research into Ai is knowledge. Machines are able to be trained to act and give off reactions that are like humans, but this is only going to happen if the computer is able to learn off an abundant amount of information that teaches them how the world works. This kind of programming needs to have a lot of information, as well as access to relations, categories, objects, and properties between all of the parts so that it can put this to good use and become more knowledgeable.

It is amazing what all of this is able to do if we can work with the technology in the proper manner.

When the program or the machine is able to implement some of the artificial intelligence that we are talking about, it will be able to initiate things like common sense, it can start with reasoning and problem solving, and can handle tasks that are really hard to do and kind of tedious, in no time at all.

We are going to explore this in a bit more information below, but machine learning is also an important part that comes with AI. Learning without any supervision is going to require us to teach the computer how to identify patterns that come in quickly with our inputs, while learning with a lot of supervision means that the computer or the machine is going to be able to learn with the help of regression that is numerical and classification.

What does all this mean though? Classification is going to be important here because it is going to help us determine the category where one object is going to belong. And then the regression is going to help us deal with obtaining a set of numerical inputs or outputs to use as examples, which then helps us to discover functions enabling the generation of suitable outputs from the inputs that we are using.

As you can see, there are a lot of different components to talk about when it comes to deep learning and artificial intelligence, and learning all of it will take a long time. but understanding some of the basics that we are talking about in this guidebook can help us to learn how these technologies are affecting our world, and even how we are able to use some of them for our own benefits as well.

Chapter 2: A Look at Machine Learning

The next topic that ewe need to spend some time exploring is the idea of machine learning. This is going to be a method of data analysis that is going to automate the analytical model building for us. It is going to fit in as one of the branches that comes with artificial intelligence because it is based on the idea that a system is able to learn from the data it receives, identify some of the different patterns that are there, and then make some decisions with a minimal amount of intervention from humans.

Because of a lot of the new technologies for computing that are available, machine learning has changed a lot in our modern world. It was born from pattern recognition and the theory that computers are able to learn without someone having to come in and program it to perform the tasks that you would like. The iterations that happen in machine learning are really important because as the models are given some more exposure to new data, they are going to be able to adapt independently. They will be able to learn from previous computations in order to produce reliable and repeatable decisions and results.

The system that is going to work with machine learning is able to learn from some of the previous computations that it went through in order to help it to get smarter. It is a type of science that is not going to necessarily be new, but it is going to be one that gains a lot of momentum in recent years.

While a lot of the algorithms out there for machine learning have been around for a very long time, the ability to automatically apply some of the mathematical calculations to the big data, at faster speeds and over and over again, is going to be a newer development. There are a lot of different applications that can come with machine learning, and this kind of technology is likely to take off steam in no time at all. Some of the most common applications that are out there that you are likely to have heard about and you may be more familiar with right now will include:

1. The self-driving car that is available through Google.
2. Online recommendation systems that we see from a lot of shopping systems like Amazon and some streaming services that you use like Netflix.
3. Knowing what the customers are saying about you on various social media accounts including Twitter.
4. Being able to detect what could potentially be fraud.

All of the new interest in machine learning is going to be due to some of the different factors that have been able to help you to do with data mining and have made this as well as the Bayesian analysis, even more popular than before. Things like the amount of data that is available, and how much and how many varieties are available than ever before. Add in that you will find that it is cheaper and more powerful and affordable to do computational processing and data storage that is affordable, it is no wonder that companies want to be able to work with the machine learning and some of the other parts that come with artificial intelligence and more.

All of these things may not mean much at first, but it does mean that it is possible to quickly and automatically produce models that are going to be able to go through a good analysis of bigger and more complex data and can deliver faster results that are more accurate than ever before. And machine learning can help you to do all of this on a scale that is much larger than ever before. And by being able to build up models that are precise, an organization is going to have a better chance of identifying some of the opportunities that are more profitable, or to avoid unknown risks that can show up.

There are going to be a few different things that need to be present in order to work with some of the systems of machine learning that will ensure they do what you would like. Some of these are going to include ensemble modeling, iterative and automation processes to get the work done, both basic and more advanced algorithms, the ability to scale, and the capabilities to prepare the data that you want to work with.

There are also a few other things that we need to know when it comes to machine learning to help us really understand how this is going to work and why machine learning is such a great part of technology that we are able to work with as well. Some of the interesting facts that we should know include:

1. When you are working with machine learning, the target is going to be known as a label.
2. When you are looking at the world of statistics, the target is going to be known as a dependent variables.
3. A variable in the world of statistics is going to be known as a feature of machine learning.
4. A transformation in statistics is going to be known as a process of feature creation when you do machine learning

Almost any kind of business that you want to run can utilize machine learning though it is sometimes expensive and time consuming so you really need to take a look at the product you have and the information you want to sort through to determine if this is actually the right option to help you out. For really competitive industries or larger companies with a ton of data, this may be the best data to look through and learn about. As you explore more with machine learning and what it is able to provide to you, you may be amazed at how many different types of companies and industries are going to rely on the ideas and the different algorithms that come with machine learning.

With this in mind, we need to take a look at some of the different methods that are popular when it comes to machine learning. The two most commonly used methods are going to be supervised machine learning and unsupervised machine learning. But there are a few other methods that come with machine learning that you are able to work with as well. Let's explore these a bit to see how they are alike and different, what they can do in machine learning, and why they are so important.

The first type of machine learning algorithm that we are going to explore is supervised machine learning. These ones are going to be trained with the help of examples that have been labeled, such as when the input is given with the desired output known. For example, you could have a piece of equipment that has some data points labeled either F for failed or R for runs. The learning algorithm is going to be able to receive a set of inputs with the outputs that are correct for them. The algorithm is going to be able to step in and learn when it compares the actual output with the correct outputs in order to find the errors that may be present.

From there, it is going to be able to modify the different model that it is using accordingly. Through methods including gradient boosting prediction ,regression, and classification, this kind of learning algorithm is going to use some patterns in order to predict the values of the label on an additional data that is unlabeled. Supervised learning is going to be used in many cases where the application is going to use historical data that can predict how likely events in the future are. For example, it is going to anticipate for a financial institution when a credit card transaction is most likely to be fraudulent or when an insurance customer is likely to file a claim.

The next type of learning that we need to take a look at here is going to be the unsupervised learning. This one is going to be the type of learning that is going to be used against a set of data that doesn't have historical labels with it. The system is going to be given the data, but it will not be told the right answer in the process. The algorithm needs to be able to figure out what the information is and what trends are there based on what it sees.

The goal with this one is to get the algorithm to explore the data and then find a structure that is inside. This kind of algorithm can often work well when you do some transactional data. For example, it is able to identify some segments of customers who have attributes in common for marketing campaigns. Or it is going to be able to look at some of the main attributes that are going to help take a large customer base and segment them out into groups that are alike or similar to each other.

There are many different types of techniques that we are able to use with this one, but some of the ones that most programmers are going to work with will include singular value decomposition, k-means clustering, nearest neighbor mapping, and self-organizing maps. These algorithms are also going to be used to segment things like recommended items, text topics, and can help us to see some of the outliers in our information.

The next kind of learning that we are going to focus on are the semisupervised learning. This is going to be a bit different than the other two that we have talked about, but can still be valuable to look through and it will use a lot of the same kinds of applications that we have seen with supervised learning.

However, this is going to be slightly different because this kind of learning algorithm is going to be able to rely on both labeled and unlabeled data to help with training. Typically, this means that it is going to use a small amount of data that is labeled and has been mixed in with a large amount of data that is not labeled at all. This is because data that is not labeled is going to be easier to get ahold of and is not as expensive as some of the other options.

There are a few different ways that you are able to work with this kind of learning and some of the options are going to include prediction, regression, and classification. It is also something that you are going to use when you find that the cost associated with labeling is too high for you to allow for training that is fully labeled. Some of the earlier examples of how this kind of machine learning algorithm would be used was when it was used to identify a face of someone on their web cam.

And finally, we can also work with a type of machine learning algorithm that is known as reinforcement learning. This is the kind that is often used with things like navigation, gaming, and robotics. With this kind of learning, the algorithm is going to discover through a process of trial and error which actions are going to provide them with the greatest rewards.

With this kind of learning, there are going to be three components that are going to be important. The first part of this is the agent, or the decision maker and learner. The second part is going to be the environment, which will be everything that the agent is able to interact with. And then the third part is the actions, which are everything that the agent is able to do. The objective in all of this is for the agent to choose the actions that are going to maximize the expected reward as much as possible over a given amount of time. the agent is going to reach the goal much faster when it is able to follow a policy that is good. So, the main goal that comes with the reinforcement learning is to learn the best policy that it needs to follow.

As you can see, each of the different types of machine learning that you are able to work with are going to be different and they are meant to handle a lot of the different parts that come with machine learning and the data analysis that you are going to work with over time. You have to figure out what kind of data you are working with, and the kind of project that you want to solve before you are able to determine which of these algorithms you will need to use.

There is a lot that you are able to do when it comes to working on machine learning. There are already a lot of different types of technologies that are going to rely on machine learning and the different algorithms that come with it. For example, if you have ever worked with a speech recognition device on your phone, or worked with a search engine, then you have worked with machine learning as well.

These are just a few of the examples of what you are able to do when it comes to the technology of machine learning. There are already a lot of examples that are out there about machine learning, and we may not even realize how much this is being used in the world around us. Add in that we are able to work with a lot of new things in the future, and there are a lot of applications and uses for this technology that have not been thought of yet, and our future with artificial intelligence and machine learning is just going to grow.

There is so much potential that can come with working with machine learning, and you are going to find that it can be brought out and used with almost any kind of artificial intelligence and advanced learning process that you want to do with a particular program. Learning how to work with machine learning and all that it entails can make some of this work a bit easier.

Chapter 3: An Introduction to Python

Now that we have had some time to look at the idea of deep learning and artificial intelligence, as well as the ever popular machine learning that is becoming more popular all of the time, it is time to take a look at some of the things that we need to know when we are working with Python. While there are a lot of different options if you want to do artificial intelligence and machine learning, but none of them are going to add the power, the ease of use, and the variety of features and libraries that you can find with Python.

There are a lot of different reasons why you would want to work with Python to help you to get done some of the machine learning algorithms, and some of the deep learning that you would like to accomplish in the process. It may be a programming language that was designed with the beginner in mind, but it has a lot of benefits that come with it, and it is going to be able to handle a lot of the powerful and complex things that you are doing with machine learning as well.

While we are going to take some time to look at the different libraries that are available with Python and how they work to handle some of the other topics that we have talked about before, we need to start out our discussion with some of the basics that come with Python, some of the benefits of choosing this coding language over some of the others that are there, and how this language is going to be able to do with machine learning.

First, let's take a look at what Python is all about. This is an object oriented programming language that is designed with the beginner in mind. In the past, many of the other coding languages can do a lot of different things that are pretty amazing, but they were often hard to learn and you had to spend a ton of time figuring them out. These would often deter those who wanted to learn because they were just too difficult and there were just too many things that would move around and may no sense to someone who was just starting out.

With Python, things were a bit different. There are a few reasons for this, but one was that the objects were based on things in real life, and allowed the user to know where they were and hold them in the same place the whole time. this made life a bit easier overall, and avoided a lot of information moving around or getting lost in the process.

In addition to this, the coding language is easy to read, being done in English, and the work that you need to do is gong to be kept to a minimum. There are no extra lines that are not necessary, and even as you read through some of the different options that we talk about in this guidebook, and some of the examples that we provide, you will find that it is easy to read through them, even before you get started and even know what they mean.

As we are talking about this though, you may be a bit nervous about using the language. Maybe it seems a bit strange that you would need to use a language that is designed for beginners to help do things like machine learning and more complicated tasks. But you will find that this language, even though it is maybe easier than some of the other languages out there, and designed with the beginner in mind, is meant to have a lot of power as well. As we go through some of the libraries below that work well with machine learning and artificial intelligence, Python is still the perfect language to help you get all of these algorithms and tasks that you want to do.

This is just the start of some of the benefits that you are going to enjoy when you decide to work with the Python coding language. Another benefit is all of the different libraries that come with this language as well. The basic library of Python is going to be pretty simple to work with, and can add in a lot of the functionality that you need with coding. This is great news, but you can take this a bit further and watch how adding some of the extensions and other libraries that are available with Python are going to increase what you can do as well. This can help with things like machine learning, mathematical equations, science, engineering, and more that the traditional library of Python may not be able to handle on its own.

The community support available with Python is something that a lot of programmers enjoy as well. Python is one of the most widely used programs in the world. Because of all the benefits that we have talked about in this chapter, many programmers, beginners and more advanced, throughout the world are using Python to handle all of their programming needs. This provides you with a great community of other individuals who are interested in helping you learn how to work with Python, answering your questions, and so much more.

It is easy to test the code. As you are working on your code, there is going to be some time when you need to be able to test out your code and make sure that it is working the way that you would like. And Python makes it easier to get this done, even as a beginner. Rather than worrying about messing up with the test, or deciding that you don't need to work on the testing at all because you don't know what you are doing, Python testing is easier, giving you the peace of mind to know that things will work when the program is done.

It works well with machine learning. And the number one biggest benefit that comes with working on Python is that it is going to work well with machine learning. There are a lot of different parts of machine learning, and often you can choose to go with another kind of coding language if you would like. But when it comes to power and ease of use, and the different libraries that work specifically well with machine learning like Python does. These are just a few of the reasons why Python is going to work so well with artificial intelligence and machine learning as well.

As you can see here, there are a lot of different benefits that come with working on Python machine learning, and Python can really be a great language that you should spend your time learning about and understanding. It is simple with a lot of power, has all of the extensions and capabilities that you are looking for when working on a programming language, and can help you to handle any of the machine learning algorithms and tasks that you would like to get done. And that is why we are going to spend more time in the rest of this guidebook exploring all of the libraries and methods that you can use to make Python work with machine learning.

Chapter 4: The Scikit-Learn Library

There are also a few different libraries that we are able to use with the help of Python that are going to ensure that we are able to do what we want in the world of machine learning. The regular library that comes with Python is not able to handle all of the functions and the algorithms that need to come with machine learning, but this is where a few of the different library extensions that come with Python can be helpful. The first library that we are going to explore in this guidebook is going to be Scikit-Learn.

We also need to take some time to learn about Scikit-learn. This is going to provide your users with a number of supervised and unsupervised learning algorithms through a consistent Python interface. We are going to take some time to learn more about Python later in this guidebook, but it is a fantastic tool that you are able to use to enhance your machine learning, and since it is for beginners, even those who have never worked with coding in the past will be able to use it.

The Scikit-learn was developed in 2007by David Cournapeau as a Google Summer of code project. This process is going to be suitable to use whether you need it commercially or academically.

Scikit-learn has been in use as a machine learning library inside of Python. It is going to come with numerous types of classification, regression, and clustering to help you get more results. Some of the algorithms that you will get to use with this system is going to include DBSCAN, k-means, random forests, support vector machines, and gradient boosting to name a few. And Scikit-learn was designed so that it would work well with some of the other popular libraries that are found on the Python code, including with SciPy and Numpy libraries.

This particular library was one that was developed to work all in Python, and then there are a few of the algorithms that work here that are more written in Cython instead. This ensures that the programmer who uses all of this is going to get some high quality performance in the process. You will find that this library has a lot of different features and parts that make it perfect for getting some of that machine learning done, and will ensure that you are going to be able to do many of the different algorithms that you want.

With this in mind, it is now time for us to focus a bit on how to set up the environment that you want to work with. You have to go through a few steps in order to figure out how to get this library installed on your computer and ready to go. Luckily this one is pretty easy to work with so you will have it up and running in no time, with all of the abilities that you want when it comes to writing out the chosen codes.

To start with, remember here that Scikit-Learn is going to work the best on newer versions of Python. It is not supported on any version that is older than Python 2.7 so if you are working on an older version, you are going to need to upgrade in order to use this particular library. Before you decide to install this library though, you also need to double check that there are two other libraries present on your system; the NumPy and the SciPy libraries as well.

These two libraries are going to be the basis of getting the Scikit-Learn library to function properly. They contain some of the functions and variables and other parts that come in the compiler that you will need to focus on as well, and can make it easier to actually get some of the work done that you want. Without these in place, it is going to be hard to get the functionality that you need from this Python library.

If you have worked with other parts of machine learning already, then these are probably already on your system and you are ready to go. If this is the first time that you are doing anything with Python or machine learning, then add in these libraries to get things started. If these are not present, then it is time to install them first because they are the basis of Scikit-Learn, and then add this into the mix as well.

The installation of all of these important libraries can be done with the help of pip. This is a type of tool that comes with Python, which means that if you have already installed Python on your system, or once you are done with the installation, then you will get pip. From here, you will be able to use the following command in order to get the scikit-learn ready to go:

pip install scikit-learn

From here the installation will be able to run and then it will complete once all of that is done. It is also possible for you to go through and use the option of conda to help install this library. The command that you will want to use to make sure that this happens is:

conda install scikit-learn

Once you notice that the installation of scikit-learn is complete, it is time to do some importation to get it over to the Python program. This step is necessary in order to use the algorithms that come with it. The good news is that the command to make this happen is going to be done. You simply need to go to your command line and type in import sklearn.

If your command is able to read through what you have written above, and there isn't an error message that shows up, then you know that this installation has been successful overall and you can start using this library as you wish. Take some time to explore around what it has to offer and just familiarize yourself with the environment, and how it is meant to work.

Don't worry too much right now that you don't know how to work with all of the library or that you don't know how all of the coding is supposed to go. This is going to come in a bit. We will spend a few chapters looking at all of the different machine learning algorithms that you are able to do with this Python library, and you will learn that even some of the more complicated tasks can become easy to work on when you use this program overall.

Chapter 5: Creating a Neural Network with Scikit-Learn

Before we start to introduce the TensorFlow library in the next chapter, we are going to take a little detour and learn a bit more about some of the things that you are able to do with the Scikit-Learn library. In particular, we are going to explore the world of neural networks, and how these can be used in order to help us to really do some amazing things with the coding that comes our way.

To start with, the neural networks that you encounter are going to be a great example of what unsupervised machine learning algorithms are going to look like. These types of networks are going to be used because they can find a lot of the different patterns that are present in the data that you go through. This can be done on a ton of different levels and in a way that is actually going to be more effective, and way faster, than what we would see with a person who looked through the data.

When we are looking at how these neural networks are going to work, each of the layers will be searched through by the algorithm to see whether or not there is some kind of pattern in the image. If the network is going through the layer and finds that it can't find a new pattern then it is going to make its prediction. But if it sees a new pattern in that one level, it will remember this information and move on to the next layer to see which patterns are going to be there. Depending on the complexity of the image and how new the neural network system is, it could take some time, and quite a few layers before the system is able to make a prediction. But it is going to get better and better at doing this the more that it practices.

At this point, there is the potential for a few things to happen and it is going to be based on how you set up this program. If the algorithm was able to go through the process that we have listed above, and it was successful at sorting through all of the different layers it would then be able to make a prediction of some sort. If the system is right with the prediction that it makes, then the system is going to remember this information and will become stronger in the future, while making better predictions as time goes on.

The reason that this works is because the neural network is using artificial intelligence, which we talked about earlier, in order to help it learn, and to make sure that there is a strong association, and one that grows, between the objects and the patterns that it is going to see. The more times that the system can come back and provide the user with the right answer, the more efficient the algorithm is going to become.

For those who have not explored all that you are able to do with machine learning and artificial intelligence, it may seem like we are talking about something that is impossible. But when we take a closer look at these neural networks and what all they are able to provide, you will be able to see how they work a bit more, and you will see that the idea of them being able to make decisions and sort through patterns and trends efficiently isn't as far fetched as it may seem.

For example, let's say that you have a goal to make one of your own programs, and you want this program to look over a picture that you add in and figure out what image is there. Through the neural networks, you will be able to go through a few different layers, and maybe many, and some of the information that the algorithm already knows, and then it can tell you that there is a car or a person or something else in the picture.

If you have been able to go through the steps properly and you know the algorithm is set up the right way, then the neural network will be able to make the right predictions that there is already a car in the picture. The program will come up with this kind of prediction based on the features that it knows belong to the car, including the license plate, the color, and more. When you are doing some of the coding that happens traditionally, this is going to be a kind of process that is almost impossible to work with. But with machine learning, and especially with the neural networks, you will find that this system is easier to work with and can be possible in no time.

As the programmer, you do need to do a bit of work. You have to provide the algorithm with a series of information so it knows what to do, and how to make good predictions. When it is all set up and ready to go, you would then step in and provide the system or the machine that you are using with an image of the car. The neural network is going to take some time, going layer by layer, to look over the picture before making a prediction.

For this process to work, the neural network would start with the very first layer, which could be something like the outside edges of the picture, or of the object that is inside. Then it would continue on with this path going through all of the other layers that are present in that image. When the program is done, it is going to be able to make a prediction about what is inside the image. If the program is able to make a good prediction, it is going to hold onto that information and it will get better at remembering that image again if it encounters another one like it.

There could potentially be a lot of different layers that come with this one, but the more layers and details that the neural network can find, the more accurately it will be able to predict what kind of car is in front of it. If your neural network is accurate in identifying the car model, it is going to learn from this lesson. It will remember some of these patterns and characteristics that showed up in the car model and will store them for use later. The next time that they encounter the same kind of car model, they will be able to make a prediction pretty quickly.

When working with this algorithm, you are often going to choose one, and use it, when you want to go through a large amount of pictures and find some of the defining features that are inside of them. For example, there is often a big use for this kind of thing when you are working with face recognition software. All of the information wouldn't be available ahead of time with this method. And you can teach the computer how to recognize the right faces using this method instead. It is also one that is highly effective when you want it to recognize different animals, define the car models, and more.

There are a lot of advantages that come with using this kind of model for machine learning. One of these advantages is that you are going to be able to do this method without having to control the statistics of the algorithm. Even if you don't have the statistics available, or you don't know how to use them, you will find that the neural networks can be used to ensure that any complex relationship that is there is going to show up. This is true between both the variables that are independent and dependent, and even if these variables are nonlinear.

With this in mind, we need to take a moment to look at some of the coding that is needed to make this kind of algorithm do what we would like. The coding that we can use to create our own neural network   includes:

```
import torch
import torch.nn as nn
import torch.nn.functional as F


class Net(nn.Module):

    def __init__(self):
        super(Net, self).__init__()
        # 1 input image channel, 6 output channels, 3x3 square convolution
        # kernel
        self.conv1 = nn.Conv2d(1, 6, 3)
        self.conv2 = nn.Conv2d(6, 16, 3)
        # an affine operation: y = Wx + b
        self.fc1 = nn.Linear(16 * 6 * 6, 120)  # 6*6 from image dimension
        self.fc2 = nn.Linear(120, 84)
        self.fc3 = nn.Linear(84, 10)

    def forward(self, x):
        # Max pooling over a (2, 2) window
```

```
x = F.max_pool2d(F.relu(self.conv1(x)), (2, 2))
# If the size is a square you can only specify a single number
x = F.max_pool2d(F.relu(self.conv2(x)), 2)
x = x.view(-1, self.num_flat_features(x))
x = F.relu(self.fc1(x))
x = F.relu(self.fc2(x))
x = self.fc3(x)
return x

def num_flat_features(self, x):
    size = x.size()[1:] # all dimensions except the batch dimension
    num_features = 1
    for s in size:
        num_features *= s
    return num_features

net = Net()
print(net)
```

This gets us to the point where we are able to go through the code and define both the backward and the forward function. This part is going to be where the gradients can be computed together, will be defined for you automatically when you use the function of autograd. From this point, it is possible to bring in the operations that you have for Tensor to get the function of forward done and ready to use.

This method is not always going to be the machine learning algorithm that you want to work with, but there are a lot of benefits that come with using it. One of the bigger issues that can show up with this is that the cost of doing the algorithm is going to be high. For some projects, and even for a lot of smaller businesses, this is just going to be too expensive and take up too much computational power to get it done.

Chapter 6: The TensorFlow Library

With that information under our belts and a little bit better understanding of how The Scikit-Learn library is meant to work, it is time to move on to the second library that we are going to focus on in this guidebook. This one is known as the TensorFlow library and it can do some amazing things in the Python language as well. So, let's take some time to explore this library and all that it can offer for us in machine learning.

Another thing that we need to take a look at here is the library that is known as TensorFlow. This is a type of framework that is going to come to us from Google and it is used when you are ready to create some of your deep learning models. This TensorFlow is going to rely on data-flow graphs for numerical computation. And it has been able to stop in and make machine learning easier than ever before.

It makes the process of acquiring the data, training some of the models of machine learning that you want to use, making predictions, and even modifying some of the future results that you see easier. Since all of these are important when it comes to machine learning, it is important to learn how to use TensorFlow.

This is a library that was developed by Google's Brain team to use on machine learning when you are doing it on a large scale. TensorFlow is going to bring together machine learning and deep learning algorithms and models and it makes them much more useful via a common metaphor. TensorFlow is going to use Python, just like what we say before, and it gives its users a front-end API that can be used when you would like to building applications, with the application being executed to a high performance C++.

Remember here that TensorFlow is able to help out with a lot of the different programming things that you need to do. It is used to help with building, training, and even running some of the neural networks that can be used, especially those that are meant to help with natural language processing, recurrent neural networks that we will talk about in a moment, and for image recognition.

With this in mind, it is time for us to take a look at not only how TensorFlow works, but how we are able to download this onto our system as well. This TensorFlow library is going to be a great one to use for many of the projects that we will discuss in this guidebook, and it comes with the APIs that you need to help with coding in Go, C++, Java, and Rust to name a few. We are going to take a look at all of the steps that you are going to need to follow in order to install this library with a Windows computer.

It is possible to install this kind of library on any kind of operating system that you would like and it is going to follow a similar kind of process to get it all done. But we are going to focus on getting it done on just one for now, the Windows system, so that we can see some of the basics that we need to

61

get this started. if you want to download this coding library on a Windows computer, you get the choice to install it with the help of either a pip or with the Anaconda extension.

To start with this, the native pip is going to be there in order to help us take the library of TensorFlow and then install it on your chosen system, without having to worry about it being on an environment or not. This may seem like a great option, and in many cases it is, but one thing that we need to remember here is that installing TensorFlow with a pip can sometimes cause other issues because it will interfere with other parts of Python that you have on the system, and that you may be using.

The good news to solve some of this is that the only thing you will need to run to get the pip to work is a single command. And after you have had a chance to get this command to work, TensorFlow is going to be installed and can be used in any manner that you would like on the system. And when this library is installed with the use of that native pip, the user is going to be given the option at this time to run the program from any of the directories that are available on their current system.

You also get the choice of installing the TensorFlow library with the help of the extension of Anaconda. To do this, you first need to make sure that you have created your own virtual environment. However, when you do look through some of the steps that come with Anaconda, you may see that it is going to still recommend that there is some form of a pip install that comes with this, rather than working with the conda install. This is usually because it is easier and can get the work done much faster.

Before we go through some of the coding that you need to use to finish this up, and before we are done with the install, we need to figure double check which version of Python is going to be used with this. It is best if you are able to go with a version of Python that is no lower than Python 3.5. This is the one that is going to have all of the latest features of Python and can be the easiest one to work with overall. And you get the benefit of using the pip 3 install during this process as well.

Another thing to consider is that there are two different versions of this library that you can work with. Their coding is pretty much the same, but it depends on which version that you would like. You can choose to go with either the CPU or the GPU version of this program based on your own preferences. The code that you need to use in order to download the CPU version of TensorFlow to use with Windows includes:

pip3 install – upgrade tensorflow

if you would like to make sure that you are installing the GPU version of the Tensorflow program, you would need to go through and use the following command to make it happen:

pip3 install – upgrade tensorflow-gpu

This is going to ensure that you are able to install TensorFlow on the Windows system that you are using. But another option that you can use to install this library so that you can use it with Python and all of your other machine learning algorithms will include being able to install it with the help of the Anaconda package.

Pip is a program that is automatically going to get installed when you get Python on your system. But the Anaconda program isn't. this means that if you would like to make sure that TensorFlow is able to get installed with the use of the Anaconda program, you first need to take the time to install this program. To do this, visit the website for Anaconda, download it from the website, and then find the instructions for installation from that same site.

Once you are done with this part and the Anaconda program is installed on your system, you should notice that there is a new package that comes with it known as conda. This is a good package that you are going to use on a regular basis and you should actually stop here for a bit and look through it. It can help you to manage your environment and more all in one place.

You can now go over to the main screen for Windows, click on the button for Start, and then choose on the tab for All Programs here we need to expand out the information and see Anaconda. You can click on the prompt for this so that it launches the Anaconda program on your system. If you wish to look through some of the details that are available on a particular package, you just need to run the command of "conda info". This is a simple code, but will give you a chance to read all of the details about the package as well as the manager for that particular package.

There is something else that you may find interesting when it comes to using the Anaconda package, and this is that it is going to help you to not rely on another virtual environment from Python, but will go through the process of helping you to create your own to use. This new environment is going to be like its own little copy of Python that is isolated, with all of the capabilities of maintaining all of the files that it needs, along with all of the paths and all of the directories. This is a great thing because you can do the work that you need in one version of Python, or any of the other libraries that you choose, without having a negative affect on some of the other projects that you may be trying to do in the process.

You will find that having one of your own virtual environments can be a great thing because they can provide the user with a method that helps to isolate projects, and you can then make sure that you avoid any of the potential problems that can show up if you are sharing an environment Note that this is an environment that is going to be different from the normal environment that you will use with Python. This is important to keep in mind because it is going to help you to get the work done, without any negative parts happening in your other projects.

At this point, we are going to work to create a virtual environment for the TensorFlow package. This can be done with the help of the conda create command. Since we are going to create an environment that is known as tensorenviron, you would use the syntax that is below:

conda create -n tensorenviron

At this point, the program is going to ask you whether or not you would like to allow the process of creating the environment to continue on, or if you would like to cancel the work that you are doing. You will want to type in the "y" and then hit the enter key to move on. This will allow the installation to continue on successfully to see the results that you want.

After you have gone through and created this kind of environment, you will need to take some time to activate it. Without the right activation, you won't be able to use this new environment that you have set up. The activation is going to be done with the help of the activate command. And then you will list out the name of the environment that you want to work with. An example of how you would pull up the environment that you just created includes:

Activate tensorenviron

Now that you have been able to activate the TensorFlow environment, it is time to go ahead and make sure that the package for TensorFlow are going to be installed too. You are able to do this by using the command below:

Conda install tensorflow

When you get to this part of the coding, your computer is going to be able to present you with a longer list of all the different types of packages that you are able to install, and it also comes with the package that is needed for TensorFlow. You will be given a prompt to decide whether you want to download it all at once, or just little parts of it at a time. You can then type in Y and hit enter on your keyboard to get the program to proceed.

Once you have gotten to this point and agreed to all of this, the installation package is going to start doing its work right away. However, notice that the process for doing this installation will take at least a few minutes, if not longer, and the amount of time that it will take to complete is going to depend on how much speed you have on your computer and with your internet provider. This can take at least a few minutes to complete so give it some time.

After the installation process is all done, you can then move on and take a few steps to check whether the installation process was a successful one or not. This is an easy process to do because you just need to go through and run the statement for importing with Python. The statement is going to be done from the Python terminal, and if you are doing this using the prompt that comes with Anaconda, then you just need to type in one word, 'python' and then hit on your enter key. This will make sure that you are going to be in the chosen terminal, and then you can go through the process of using the code below to help continue on:

Import tensorlow as tf

If you find that the package wasn't installed in the proper manner, you are going to end up with an error message on the screen after you do this code. If you don't see an error message, then you know that the installation of the package was successful.

Chapter 7: K-Nearest Neighbors and K-Means Clustering

In this chapter, we are going to spend some time looking at two of the different algorithms that you are able to work with in order to help do a few different processes with Python machine learning. These two that are the focus of our coding will include the K-Nearest Neighbors, or KNN, and the K-Means clustering. These are two popular algorithms that you are able to work with, and knowing how to use them, when they can be beneficial, and more can be critical to helping you to really see some results.

First, we are going to take a look at KNN. This one is going to be used to take some of the data that you present and search through it for the k most similar examples of any kind of instance that you would like to work with. When this is done, then the algorithm is going to look through all of the data, even if you have a lot of data, in order to help you have a summary of it all. Then the algorithm can take the results that it provides to you in order to make predictions for you.

Any time that you decide to work with this particular model, you may find that the learning is going to work well because it becomes really competitive. The reason that this is helpful is because there is going to be some competition that happens between the various parts of the algorithm, or even the different elements, in the various models so that you can end up with the best predictions based on any data that you have.

As you get to working on the KNN algorithm, you will notice that it is a bit different compared to some of the other algorithms that we are going to discuss in this guidebook. For example, in some cases programmers would consider this as a lazier approach to learning because it isn't going to actually go through and create a model for you, at least not until you actively go in and make a new prediction.

Depending on what kind of situation you are trying to work on with that information, this can sometimes be a good thing for your project. This ends up being beneficial because waiting to make new predictions is going to help you to have data that is always up to date, or at least data that you want inside the algorithm. This ensures that you are not going to end up with predictions that are not valid or useful for what you need.

If you had this program work in a different manner, such as having it do predictions at regular intervals, or each time that you inserted some new data, it could be helpful if the situation needed it. But then there are times when you want to just look at a specific customer group or certain information, and this constant updating is not going to be good for what you need The KNN algorithm will make sure that the updates and the new predictions only happen when you want them to.

You will find as you work with this kind of algorithm that there are a number of benefits to using it. When you do bring out the KNN algorithm, you are going to find that it is easier to cut through some of the noise that shows up in the set of data. This noise is sometimes really loud if you are working through a ton of data, and getting rid of some of that noise, especially when it starts to get really distracting, can make it easier to look at the information and the data in front of you and see what trends and patterns are actually there, and what you are able to do with them.

In addition, if your company is trying to deal with and sort through a lot of data at the same time, then the KNN algorithm is going to be the best choice for you. Unlike a few of the other algorithms that are in this guidebook or some of the other ones that you may read about, this algorithm is going to work well because there are no limits on the data size that it is able to sort through.

However, there are going to be a few potential issues that can come up when you are working with this algorithm. To start with the costs of computation are going to be much higher. This is even more true when you try to compare it to some of the other algorithms that could handle similar or the same kind of work. The reason that the costs here are going to turn up higher is because the algorithm will take all of the data, and then sort through every little point that it can, rather than trying to cluster them and send over a prediction.

When the system has to actually look at each individual point, and in large sets of data that could be millions of points, it is going to take a lot of power and time and this is where the extra costs will come in. after this section we will take a look at the K-Means clustering and see why the clustering process can sometimes be a beneficial choice.

With that said, the KNN algorithm can be a great one for you to use in order to see some great benefits with your work and to help you really sort out all of the different data points and information that you have, even when the set of data is really large and seems impossible to go through.

Learning the steps that we will go through below will make sure that you are set up and ready to work with this machine learning algorithm.

How does the K-Nearest algorithm work

Now that we have taken a few minutes to discuss this kind of algorithm and all that can come with it, it is time to take a look at some of the steps that you need to follow to make sure that you can use the KNN algorithm in the proper manner. Some of the best steps to use to get started with the KNN algorithm are going to include:

1. Load the data into the algorithm for it to read through.
2. Initialize the value that you are going to use and rely on for k.
3. When you are ready to get the predicted class, iteration from one to total number of the data points that you use for training, you can use the following steps to help.
    a. Start by calculating the distance that is in between each of your test data,

and each row of your training data. We are going to work with the Euclidean distance as our metric for distance since it's the most popular method. Some of the other metrics that you may choose to work with here include the cosine and Chebyshev.
b. Sort the calculated distances going in ascending order, based on their distance values.
c. Get the k rows from the sorted array.
d. Get the most frequent class for these rows.
e. Return back the class prediction.

The K-means clustering

The next algorithm that we are going to spend some time looking at is known as the k-means clustering. This is a basic idea that is found with a lot of different kinds of algorithms in this topic, but this is one of the easiest, and most common, forms of clustering that you are able to work with.

It is also a good example of unsupervised machine learning as well. It is going to be applied in most cases when the data that you have doesn't come with labels that are on it. The goal of working with this algorithm to ensure that you can see the clusters or the groups that are found inside your data.

The whole point of these clusters is that the objects that are found in the same cluster are going to be closely related to the other points that fall into that same cluster. In addition, these points are not going to have as many similarities to the items that are found in any other cluster that you set up. The similarity here is going to be a metric used to see how strong the relationship between the objects are in the set of data.

There are a variety of times when you would use this kind of clustering, but one example is when you are doing the process of data mining, especially if the data mining is more exploratory. It could also have uses in other kinds of fields, including some that have to go with compressing data, image analysis, computer graphics, pattern recognition, and machine learning to list out a few.

When you use this kind of algorithm, it is going to help you to form up some of the data clusters that you need, based on the values that come with your data. As a programmer, it is then your job to go through and specify out what you want the value of k to end up being. This means that you need to determine how many clusters you would like the algorithm to make out of the data. The algorithm is then going to take the value of K and use it to select the centroid value for all of the clusters that you are working with.

When the steps above are done, it is then time for the k-means algorithm to go through and complete three more steps. These steps are going to include:

1. You will want to start with the Euclidian distance between each data instance and the centroids for all of the clusters.
2. Assign the instances of data to the cluster of centroid with the nearest distance possible.

3. Calculate the new centroid values, depending on what the mean values of the coordinates of the data instances from the corresponding cluster.

Writing out the formula for K-means clustering

So the first step that we will need to do is to calculate the cluster responsibilities. The formula we will use is the following:

r(kn) = exp[-b * d(m(k), x(n))] / sum[j=1..K] { exp[-b * d(m(j), x(n))] }

From here, you can see that the r(k,n) is going to work out as a fraction, some number that is in between 0 and 1, where you can interpret the hard k-means or the regular k-means to be the case where r(k,n) is always exactly equal to 0 or 1. The d(*,*) can be any valid distance metric, but the Euclidean or squared Euclidean distances are the ones that are used the most.

Then for the second step, we are going to work on a formula that is similar to the hard k-means, but we are just recalculating the means based on the responsibilities that we want to sent with it. The algorithm that we are going to use for this includes:

m(k) = sum[n=1..N] { r(k,n)* x(n)] / sum[n-1..N] { r(k,n) }

so, when you take the time to look at this algorithm above, you are going to see that it is similar to the weighted mean. This is going to show you that if the r(k,n) is higher, then the mean is going to be more important to the cluster of k. When you see this, it is going to show that this is going to have the biggest influence on the calculation of the mean. But if the mean is higher when you look at the algorithm, you will know that the opposite is true.

Now, with some of the information in order that we have discussed already, it is time to look at some of the coding that is needed in order to create one of our own K-Means clustering algorithms, and how to add in some of the soft k-means to any code that you would like to work with. Some of the coding that you need to make this happen includes:

```
import numpy as np
import matplotlib.pyplot as plt


def d(u, v):
    diff = u - v
    return diff.dot(diff)


def cost(X, R, M):
    cost = 0
    for k in xrange(len(M)):
        for n in xrange(len(X)):
            cost += R[n,k]*d(M[k], X[n])
    return cost
```

After this part, we are going to take the time to define your function so that it is able to run the k-means algorithm before plotting the result. This is going to end up with a scatterplot where the color will represent how much of the membership is inside of a particular cluster. We would do that with the following code.

```
def plot_k_means(X, K, max_iter=20, beta=1.0):
    N, D = X.shape
    M = np.zeros((K, D))
    R = np.ones((N, K)) / K

    # initialize M to random
    for k in xrange(K):
        M[k] = X[np.random.choice(N)]

    grid_width = 5
    grid_height = max_iter / grid_width
    random_colors = np.random.random((K, 3))
    plt.figure()

    costs = np.zeros(max_iter)
    for i in xrange(max_iter):
        # moved the plot inside the for loop
        colors = R.dot(random_colors)
```

```
        plt.subplot(grid_width, grid_height, i+1)
        plt.scatter(X[:,0], X[:,1], c=colors)

        # step 1: determine assignments / resposibilities
        # is this inefficient?
        for k in xrange(K):
            for n in xrange(N):
                R[n,k] = np.exp(-beta*d(M[k], X[n])) / np.sum( np.exp(-beta*d(M[j], X[n])) for j in xrange(K) )

        # step 2: recalculate means
        for k in xrange(K):
            M[k] = R[:,k].dot(X) / R[:,k].sum()

        costs[i] = cost(X, R, M)
        if i > 0:
            if np.abs(costs[i] - costs[i-1]) < 10e-5:
                break

    plt.show()

def main():
```

```
# assume 3 means
D = 2 # so we can visualize it more easily
s = 4 # separation so we can control how far apart the means are
mu1 = np.array([0, 0])
mu2 = np.array([s, s])
mu3 = np.array([0, s])

N = 900 # number of samples
X = np.zeros((N, D))
X[:300, :] = np.random.randn(300, D) + mu1
X[300:600, :] = np.random.randn(300, D) + mu2
X[600:, :] = np.random.randn(300, D) + mu3

# what does it look like without clustering?
plt.scatter(X[:,0], X[:,1])
plt.show()

K = 3 # luckily, we already know this
plot_k_means(X, K)

# K = 5 # what happens if we choose a "bad" K?
# plot_k_means(X, K, max_iter=30)
```

```
# K = 5 # what happens if we change beta?
# plot_k_means(X, K, max_iter=30, beta=0.3)


if __name__ == '__main__':
    main()
```

Clustering algorithms can be really useful when it comes to working with machine learning and some of the other choices that come with computer sciences, and the k-means clustering is a great way to gain some experience with doing all of this and ensuring that you are going to get everything matched up and working the way that you would like. Make sure to learn some of the equations above, and some of the benefits of these carious algorithms, so that you can use them for your computing needs when necessary.

Chapter 8: Decision Trees and Random Forests in Machine Learning

The next kind of machine learning algorithm that we are going to look at are going to include the decision tree and the random forest. These work together because a bunch of decision trees can make up a random forest. These are great tools to use when you need to see which decision is the best for your company, and you want to compare and contrast the different decisions that you are able to make. let's first explore a bit more what these decision trees are all about, and then we can dive into some more about how they work together to make up a random forest.

To start with the decision tree is going to be a good tool for data and can be efficient if you would like to take a look at more than one choice, and you know the choices are going to be completely different. You can gather up information on both choices and put them into the decision tree to help make the right decision to improve and even to grow your business. When the different options are presented through the decision tree to you, you can use this to see what the potential outcomes of each decision will be in the future. This makes it much easier to make accurate and smart decisions and can help with predictions in the future as well.

As a programmer or even a business owner who wants to use this kind of algorithm, there are a few options when it comes to how you would work with these decision trees. Many of those who are using it are going to use it to help with random or categorical variables. In many cases though, machine learning is going to want you to make these trees as a classification problem.

To help you double check that any decision tree you are making ends up being a good one, you will need to be able to take up all of the sets of data that you want to work with, and then you need to be able to split them up between two, and often more, sets with similar data being found in each of the sets. These can then be sorted out with the help of the independent variables that you can choose from, simply because this ensures that each set is distinguished and set out from all the others.

So, now that we have gotten to this part, it brings up the idea that this can be something that is hard to work on. In order to make sure that the decision tree is going to work the way that you would like, or to at least see how it is going to behave when you try to use it, let's look at a good example of this. In this one, we are going to have a group with 60 people inside of it.

With these people, all of them are going to have three independent variables. These variables are going to include the height of the person, their gender, and what class they are in. Then, when it is time to look at the students who are in that group, you will be able to find out that half of them like to play soccer as well. Using the independent variables that you were presented above, your goal is to figure out which half of the students like to play soccer, and which ones do not like to play this sport.

Going from the information that you have about which kinds of students are the most likely to enjoy playing soccer, you decide that it is time to create a model to help you look at that group of 60 people and decide which 30 out of them like the game of soccer, and which 30 are going to spend their time playing or doing something else.

To make this one work the model needs to be able to go through all of the students who are in the group, or all of the people in your group, and then divide them up into two groups. You need to have a group that is going to be the ones that are going to love playing soccer, and the ones that don't. and you want to make sure that the model is as accurate as possible.

There are some other possibilities that you can work with that work well with the decision tree. These algorithms are useful because it is going to help you to split up all of the data that you have, providing a few different subsets that are going to give you good outcomes that are the most homogenous, and will ensure that all of the decisions that you make based on this information is as accurate as possible. Remember here that you can have more if the situation needs it, but for the example that we are doing here, you will only want to work with two subgroups and no more.

You may find that there are a lot of times when a business or another company will need to go through some data that is complex and they want to use this information to make decisions and figure out what actions they should take. A decision tree is going to help them to get this done and to provide them with the data they need in an efficient and helpful manner

In the past before working with some of the various machine learning algorithms, like decision trees, a business owner would need to work with their own intuition in order to make their decisions. But the world is much more complex now, and there is a ton of extra information that is out there that is hard to sort through on your own. Relying on some of these algorithms and systems to help you to make your decisions, rather than just guessing and risking a lot of time and money can make a big difference.

Moving to the random forest

Now that we have had some time to explore what the decision tree is all about, it is time to move on to another step of looking at the random forest. There are times when just one single decision tree is going to be enough to help you make some decisions for your needs. But sometimes, you need to compare a lot of different options and you are going to need to work with a group of decision trees, which will make up your own random forest.

These random forests are going to be a popular option to work with when we talk about machine learning. So, if you plan to work with decision trees on machine learning quite a bit, then it is also important to learn how to work with the random forests as well.

Since the random forest algorithm is so popular with a lot of programmer, it is not going to be hard for you to see that it could potentially help you with a lot of different types of problems. For example, if you are looking to work with some tasks that can look through and explore the data that you have, and deal with values that are missing, or you would like to deal with some of the outliers that show up in the data that is there.

There are a lot of times when you are going to be able to use the random forest to help with various parts of machine learning. The random forest is going to be the best way to provide you with results out of complex or large amounts of data. And often this algorithm is going to be able to do a much better job than what you may see with some of the other algorithms that we will talk about in this guidebook. With this in mind, some of the advantages that you can get for working with random forests include:

- When you are working on your own training sets, you will find that all of the objects that are inside a set will be generated randomly, and it can be replaced if your random tree things that this is necessary and better for your needs.

- If there are M input variable amounts, then m<M is going to be specified from the beginning, and it will be held as a constant. The reason that this is so important because it means that each tree that you have is randomly picked from their own variable using M.

- The goal of each of your random trees will be to find the split that is the best for the variable m.

- As the tree grows, all of these trees are going to keep getting as big as they possibly can. Remember that these random trees are not going to prune themselves.

- The forest that is created from a random tree can be great because it is much better at predicting certain outcomes. It is able to do this for you because it will take all prediction from each of the trees that you create and then will be able to select the average for regression or the consensus that you get during classification.

Before you decide that the random forests are going to be the right tool for you, it is important to remember that they do have some negatives. For example, they are able to help you handle some of the regression problems that come your way, but they will not be able to make predictions past whatever kind of training data you decide to add into it, or the ranges that you are working with when you submit the information.

What this means is that the random forests are going to help you to make some predictions, and they will be the best part of helping you to make some decisions that work well for your business. While there are a lot of benefits that come with it, there are also going to be some limitations because of how far in the future it is able to make the predictions. This lowers the amount of accuracy that you have. Depending on what you are trying to learn about though, you may find that this algorithm is still one of the best for your needs.

Chapter 9: The Linear Classifier and What This Means

As you are going through some of the different parts that come with supervised machine learning algorithms, you may find that two of the most common tasks that you will need to focus on will include either the linear classifier or the linear regression to get things done. The linear regression is useful because it helps you to predict what values you will get, while the linear classifier is that it is going to focus on the class specifically. We are going to take a look at the linear classifier in particular in this chapter, and how you can use it with some of your machine learning.

You will find that when you are trying to use the libraries we talked about earlier in this guidebook to do some machine learning work, that the classification problems are going to take up the majority of your work, often 80 percent of the machine learning tasks that you need to do. The classification is going to aim at predicting how probable it is going to be for each class to occur given the set of inputs that you would need to add in. The label, which is going to be known as our variable that is dependent in this case, is going to be the class, or the discrete value.

If the dependent variable, or our label, is going to work with just two classes in the process, then you know that the learning algorithm you choose is going to be a binary classifier in the end. But if you are working on a classifier that is more multiclass, this means that it is going to be able to tackle the labels that have two classes or more.

Let's look at an example of this. Many times the classification problems that we are working on that turn out to be binary will be able to help you predict the likelihood that your customer is going to come back to the business again and make another purchase. But if you want to work with a system that is going to make some predictions about the type of animal that shows up in a given picture, then you are working with what is known as a multiclass classification problem because there will be more than two varieties of animals that the program has to deal with.

With this in mind, it is time to measure out the performance of linear classifier that you can work with. Accuracy is one of the best topics to start with here. The performance overall of this classifier is going to be measured by how accurate it can be. Accuracy is able to collect all of the values that are correct that you have, and then it will be able to divide that number by the total number of observations that are present.

Let's say that you have a value of accuracy in the algorithm or the data that you are working with that is about 85 percent. What this is going to mean for you is that when you put that model to use, it is going to provide you with an answer that is right about 85 percent of the time. it will also be incorrect 15 percent of the time. The goal with this one, of course, is to keep the percentage of being correct as high as possible.

At this point, you can already see that there may be a bit of a shortcoming that comes with it when you work on that metric, especially if you are doing a class that includes some imbalance. A set of data that is not balanced very well is going to happen when the amount of observations that show up is not going to be equal in all of the groups that you are working with.

To take this further, let's say that you are working on a classification problem of a rare event with your function of logistics. You can imagine here that the classifier that you are using is going to try and estimate how many patients died when they contracted one kind of disease. In the data that you have, about five percent of the patients who contract this disease are going to pass away from that kind of disease.

With this information in mind, you can then go through and train the classifier to make sure that it can make a god prediction about the number of deaths that end up happening, and then you can work with the accuracy metric in order to evaluate the performance of that hospital or that clinic. Now, if the classifier is able to work and predicts that there are 0 deaths for the whole set of the data, then it is going to show that this model is right about 95 percent of the time when used.

From here, we need to move on and take a look at what is going to be called the confusion matrix. This is one of the better ways available for us to look at the performance of the classifier compared to the accuracy. When you are working with one of these confusion matrix, you will get the benefit of visualizing how the accuracy metric of the classifier is going to be when it is compared to the predicted, and the actual classes that you choose. The binary confusion matrix is going to have a series of four squares and the parts that you are able to see in this kind of matrix is going to include:

1. TP: This is going to known as the true positive. This is going to contain all of the predicted values that were correctly predicted as an actual positive.

2. FP: This is going to be the false ones, or the ones that were predicted in an incorrect manner. They were usually predicted as positive, but they were actually negative. This means that the negative values show up, but they had been predicted ahead of time as positive.
3. FN: This is false negative. This is when your positive values were predicted as negative.
4. TN: this is going to be the true negative. These are the values that were predicted in a correct manner and were predicted as actual negative.

When you take a look at one of these of these confusion matrix, you will be able to see a clear look at the actual class and the predicted class and see what is going on there.

The next thing that we want to focus on here is how to look at the precision and how sensitive this algorithm can be. You will see that when you create one of your own confusion matrix, there is a lot of information that is going to show up. It is also going to be useful to help us to see some good insights into any of the true and the false positives that will show up here. But, there are also some case where it is preferable to have a metric that is a bit more concise than what we have been talking about so far.

To help us out with this, we first need to take some time to look at the precision that comes with the code. This precision metric is going to give us the amount of accuracy that shows up in the positive class. This just means that it comes into play to give us an idea, as well as the measure, or how likely that the prediction of the positive class is actually correct. To help you check this in your own matrix, you will need to use the following code:

Precision = TP/(TP + FP)

The maximum score that you can get here is one. And this is going to show up the classifier perfectly comes up correctly with the positive values. Precision alone is not going to be that helpful because it is going to ignore the negative class. This matric is something that you may want to pair up with the recall metric. The recall is also called sensitivity or true positive rate.

The next thing that we need to take a look at is the sensitivity. This sensitivity is important because it is going to help us compute the ratio of positive classes that the algorithm was able to detect correctly. This metric can be a good way to model and take a look at a positive class. The formula for figuring out the sensitivity is:

Recall = TP/(TP + FN)

How to use the linear classifiers in TensorFlow

Remember earlier how we talked about TensorFlow and all that can come with it. But now it is time to take this a bit further and look at how you are actually able to work with TensorFlow, and how you can really do some great things with machine learning through this Python library.

Now it is time for us to take a look at some of the practical work that we are able to do with the linear classifiers through the TensorFlow library. We are going to take an example of how to work with this using the census data. The purpose of us going through these steps is to make sure that you use a variable in the census data set in order to make sure that we can take a look at the participants we have and can make predictions on how much income they make. note that the income is going to become our variable that is binary for this example.

For this one to work, we are going to set the binary variable to be at one when the individual has an income that is higher than $50,000 a year. But if you have a participant with an income per year that is less than the $50,000, then they are going to have the variable show up as 0. The set of data that we will work with here can be separated out into variables that are categorical, and there are eight of them. These will include the following:

Native country

Sex
Race
Relationship
Occupation
Marital status
Education
And place of work

And on top of this, we are going to take a look in this at six of the continuous variables. These are going to include:

Hours_week
Capital_loss
Capital_gain
Education_num
Fnlwgt
Age

With this information, we can bring up the TensorFlow extension to help us to figure out the probability to see which of our customers, or any individuals in the set of data, are going to fit into the two groups that we set up. These people are going to be separated out into the two groups that we set up before (although you can add in as many groups as you would like based on what kind of program you are doing). IN this one, the two groups will be based on whether the individuals make above or under the $50,000 a year.

When this is done, you will be able to look into the groups that were formed and find out some of the background information that is there, including what gender, their race, where they live, what their occupation is, and so much more. This is a kind of tool that a lot of businesses are turning to and starting to rely on more than ever because it helps them to learn about new and potential customers, as well as repeat customers, and can make their marketing more efficient overall.

What are the differences between discriminative and generative models?

As we are working on some of the parameters that are found with our linear classifier, there are going to show up two separate classes or methods that we need to work with, which are going to be broad at this time, and are meant to help you figure out how to determine where the parameters should be set. The options that you have here are going to be the generative or the discriminative model.

Methods that fit in with the generative model are going to be considered conditional density functions. The two biggest examples that you are going to see of this kind of algorithm is going to be something like the linear discriminant analysis. This is going to be like the Naïve Bayes Classifier or the Gaussian conditional density models.

Then a programmer also gets the choice of working with what is known as the discriminative model. These are important because they are set up to work so that your output will come out as high quality as possible when you do a new set of training. Additional terms in the training can be necessary, but these will cost more overall and could perform what is known as regularization of your final model. The good news is that this model is going to provide you with a few options to make it easier to work with, and these options are going to include the following:

1. Logistic regression. This is going to be the likelihood estimation of linear classifiers assuming that the observed training set was generated by a binomial model that depends on the output of the classifier.
2. Perceptron: This is a type of algorithm that you are going to use because it will try to go through and fix up any and all of the errors that can occur in a training set.
3. Support vector machine: This is one of the options that we talked about before. It is going to be the algorithm that will be able to maximize, as much as possible, the margin that can come between the examples that re in the training set and the decision hyperplane.

Despite the look of the name there, the LDA is not going to belong to the discriminative models in this method. However, the nae does make sense when you are able to compare it to some of the other algorithms that are there, such as with principal components analysis. You will find that the LDA algorithm is going to fit in with supervised learning and it is going to be able to utilize the labels on your data, but the PCA is going to be an algorithm of unsupervised learning, and it purposely goes through and ignores the labels that are present.

As you work with discriminative training, it is easy to find that it can provide you with more of the accuracy that we were talking about before compared to working with the conditional density function. If you are looking to get a higher amount of accuracy out of the work that you are doing, then this is the best algorithm to work with.

However, there are some issues that can come up with it as well. While the discriminative training is going to provide you with some more accuracy along the way, the conditional density models are able to handle some of the missing data points in an easier manner. If your data is missing in a lot of places, or you are concerned about how that missing data is going to affect your predictions, then going with the conditional density models is the best option.

Working with linear classifiers can be a great way to work with some more of the things that we have already talked about with machine learning, while also giving you some more time to learn about and actually use the TensorFlow library as we talked about before. Take some time to work through the equations that we provided above and see just how these linear classification problems can be handled.

Chapter 10: Are Recurrent Neural Networks Different From Neural Networks

We spent some time talking about the neural networks before and how they can work to make predictions and can get stronger the more times they are exposed to inputs and can learn from them. Now we are going to take that a bit further and discuss another topic that is along the same lines, the idea of recurrent neural networks.

When we are doing a study of the human brain, it is reasonable to know that when we think, this process isn't going to restart from nothing every few seconds. We are going to keep building on what we were able to learn in the past. We remember what we learned as a child, or even yesterday when we went through a new process. And we can retain that information for a long time to come. We don't have to relearn how to brush our teeth each day, we just remember how to do that so we can focus on learning new things in the future. This is important because it is going to tell us that the thoughts we have are going to have persistence and consistency that goes along with them.

With those traditional neural networks from before, you won't see this same kind of process occurring, and sometimes this is going to be a shortcoming that we need to work for. For example, if you would like to be able to go through and classify a kind of event that is happening at different points in the movie, this would be something that the regular neural network that we talked about before would struggle with a bit.

The good thing to remember here is that there is a machine learning algorithm that is able to handle this, and that is the recurrent neural networks. These networks are going to have what are known as loops in them, which makes it easy for the information that it learns to persist, much like it does in the human brain. In this method, the loop is going to be take all of the information that you have and will pass it from one part of your network over to the next. This is going to be similar to what would happen if you had more than one copy of the same network, with each message getting moved on over to the successor has time went on.

This chain like nature is important because it is going to show us how the recurrent neural networks are going to be related pretty closely to the sequences and the lists. They are the natural architecture of the neural network to use for the data. And they will be used on a frequent basis when it comes to machine learning. In the last few years, there has been a lot of people working with these and trying to see how much success they were able to garner from using these kinds of networks.

One of the limitations that come with the recurrent neural networks that is pretty glaring is that the API is going to come with a variety of constraints you have to work through. They are only going to be able to take an input of a fixed sized vector, and they are only able to produce an output that is in a fixed sized vector as well. These models are going to also perform the mapping that you want, but they can only do it within a fixed number of computational steps, which is going to equal the number of layers that you are going to see in the model.

The main reason that these recurrent neural networks are going to be useful and can actually be exciting to use in your coding is that they will allow you as the programmer to operate your own work over a sequence of vectors, rather than just one. This is going to include having these sequences in the input, the output, but oftentimes you will find them in both of these places.

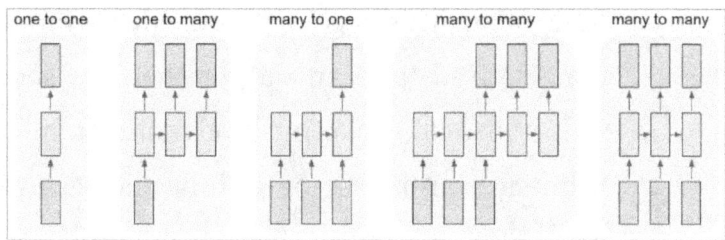

To help us see how these recurrent neural networks are going to work, we need to take a look at the charts above to give us an example. Each of those rectangles above are going to be one of our vectors, and then the arrows are going to be the parts that tell us the functions. The input with the vectors are going to be the ones that are red, and ten the output vectors that we need to know are the ones that show up in blue. You can also see that there are some green vectors present as well ans these are going to hold onto what is known as the state of the RNN. Going from the left diagram over to the right with what is above, let's see how each one is going to work and gain a better understanding of these recurrent neural networks.

1. The first one is going to be the vanilla mode of processing, the one that doesn't use the RNN at all. This is going to include an input that is fixed, and an output that is fixed. This is also known as image classification.
2. Sequence output is going to be the second part. This is going to be image captioning that is able to take an image and then will provide you with an output of a sentence of words.

3. Sequence input: This is goi going to be the third picture above. It is going to be more of a sentiment analysis that shows us a given sentence and makes sure that it is classified as either a negative or positive sentiment.
4. Sequence output and sequence output. You can find this one in the fourth box, and it is getting a bit closer to what we want. This one is going to be similar to a machine translation. This is when the RNN is able to read a sentence out in English, and then can take that information and provide you with an output that reads the sentence in rench.
5. And finally, the last box is going to be the synced sequence input and output. The video classification here is going to help us to label out each of the frames that occur in a video if we decide to.

Notice that in each of these, there aren't going to be any constraints put on the lengths of the sequences that we have to specify ahead of time. this is because the recurrent transformation, which is going to be shown in green, is fixed, and we are able to apply it out as many times as we would like, or as many times as work with our project.

Looking at how the RNN algorithm is going to work.

We will now take some time to look at an example of how this kind of algorithm is really going to be able to work for us. In this particular example, we will work to train this algorithm at the mode for the character level language. What this is going to mean is that we are going to provide the RN with a lot of text, and then we are going to ask it to give us a model about the probability of distribution for the next character that should show up in that sequence.

The answer is going to be based on the previous characters that we see. This is a good project to work on because it shows us how the RNN algorithm is going to be able to generate a new text for us, even though it is finding the text with one character at a time.

So, with our program, we are going to assume that we had a really limited and we only had four possible letters to work with. With just this limited amount of information, we want to be able to train our RNN to do a sequence so that it can list out the word of "hello" for us. This training sequence is going to need to include four training examples to see the results. This can sound complex when we first start but we can go through this one step at a time to hep us get a better idea of how this works and to get the letters to show up at the right time and in the right order. Some of the things that we can do to get this to happen will include:

1. The probability of getting "e" should be just as likely to occur as getting the letter "h".
2. "L should be likely in the context of "he"
3. The "l" should also be likely if the system is given the context of "hel"
4. "o" should be likely if the other sequences have happened and the context of "hell" is in place.

With this idea, we are going to take a moment to encode all of the characters that can show up in the vector working with the 1 of k encoding. We will then be able to feed this into the algorithm for RNN that we are working with, one at a time using the right function to get this to happen.

After we have been able to get all of the different parts in place, we are going to be able to observe a sequence of four dimensional output vectors, with one dimension that will show up for each of the characters, which we can then interpret at the confidence that the RNN is able to assign right now to each of the characters that come up in the next sequence at the time. One thing that is going to help us to understand how this can work is with the chart below.

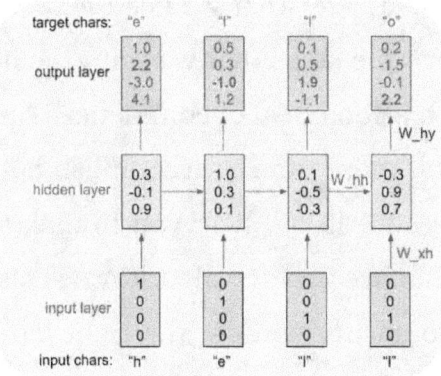

Out of this, we may use an example of seeing that in the first time step, the RNN would see the character of "h" it was able to assign some confidence to this of 1.0, to the next letter turning into "h", 2.2 to getting the letter "e" -3.0 to "l" "and 4.1 to "o". Sine the training data that we are using, (which is the string of hello that we talked about above), had the next right character being "e" we want to increase the confidence, or the green color, and then decrease how confident it is in all of the other letters, which are going to be shown in the red above.

In addition to these steps, we are going to be able to take another step here and then come up with the target character that we need here at ever one of our four time steps that we want the network to assign with a good deal of confidence. This is going to take a bit more time to accomplish but it can be helpful because it will help you to make sure that your confidence in the algorithm is as high as possible to ensure you get the right letters in the word to show up at the right time.

Sine we are working with this kind of algorithm, and it is going to be set up to include differentiable operations, we are going to be able to use what is known as the back propagation algorithm. This algorithm is going to include a recursive application of the chain rule that you may have learned in calculus. We will also be able to use this rule to help us figure out what direction we want to use to adjust the various weights at play. This ensures that we are able to increase the scores of the correct targets which in this example will be the bold and the green numbers

After you have had a chance to do this, it is time to work on the parameter update. This parameter update is going to help us to just nudge over all of the weights a bit, in whichever direction works the best for you. If we are able to double check that the inputs we feed into this algorithm are the same after each of the updates that come with the parameter, we are going to find that the scores of our correct characters would be higher, in this case being between 2.2 and 24, and then the incorrect characters that we do not want to show up will go down for us.

Since we are working on a whole word here, it is likely that we will need to repeat this process more than one time, and often main times, in order to get it to work. How many times you need to do this will often depend on the amount of complexity that comes with the system. We are keeping this pretty easy with just one word, but if you were trying to do a whole paragraph, a whole page, or even a longer document, the number of times you have to go through this would be more difficult.

Since machine learning is going to be a programming technique that has to learn over time, you may need to go through the loop and help it to learn here. Make sure that you are repeating the process until you are able to get this RNN to converge and the predictions end up being consistent with the training data. When this happens, the right characters are going to be predicted in the same and correct order, every time that you decide to run this program.

We can also work with an explanation that is a bit more technical here. And we are able to do this once we work with the standard Softmax classifier, which is sometimes referred to as the cross entropy loss) on every output vector at the same time. you will be able to train the RNN with the mini-batch Stochastic Gradient Descent, and you may find that working with Adam or RMSProp to make sure that the updates are as stable as possible.

When you do all of this, you should notice that the first time that the character of "l" is inputted to this, the target is "l" but the second time the target is going to be "o". The RNN is not going to be able to just rely on the input on its own, and it is going to need to bring in some recurrent connection to help keep track of the context that is needed to make this task achievable.

When you get to testing time, you will be able to go in and feed the right characters into the RNN algorithm. And once that is put in, you should be able to see the distribution over what characters the system is going to bring out next, and see if you get the answers that you want. We will then be able to sample from the distribution that we are given, and then we feed it all right back in to see which letter you are going to get next. You can then just repeat this process until you get everything in the right order, and you will find that you are sampling the text.

As this chapter took some time to point out, the RNN algorithm can be useful and can help you out with a lot of different projects and even problems in machine learning that you just wouldn't be able to do with some of the other algorithms we have discussed before. It will open up more doors and different opportunities to make sure that you can handle more of the situations that you want in machine learning in the process.

Chapter 11: What Else Can I Do with Python Programming and Machine Learning?

We have spent some time in this guidebook talking not only about the Python program, but also about machine learning, artificial intelligence, and deep learning. And the majority of what we have discussed is the different algorithms that you are able to use in order to actually complete some of your own programs in machine learning, of course with the help of the Python programming language.

There are a lot of different machine learning algorithms that you are able to use, and they often work with the various libraries that we have already been able to discuss in this guidebook. Learning how to work on these and why they are important, and when to bring them out for your project, can make machine learning that much easier overall.

With this in mind, there are a ton of other algorithms that work with both Python and machine learning that you are able to focus on, and this chapter is going to discuss a few of them. While we are not going to have time to dive into each and every algorithm that is available for machine learning (and there are always more being developed over time as machine learning grows and becomes even more popular), we are going to take some time to look at a few more of the Python machine learning algorithms that you should know.

Naïve Bayes

The first of these additional machine learning algorithms that we are going to focus on is known as the Naïve Bayes. To help us get a better understanding of the steps that are needed to make this one work properly, we may need to use our imaginations and think about a scenario. Imagine that you are currently working on a project that is meant to be a classification problem, but your goal here is to make sure that you are creating a hypothesis that is new and will actually work with the algorithm that you want. You also want to make sure that any design that you are handling will allow you to have a new discussion or a new feature based on how important each of your variables turns out to be.

While in the beginning this is going to seem like it is a lot of work, and like we are trying to stuff it in all at once, it is something that you are able to do with machine learning. Once you can take some time in order to collect all of the different information that you need, it is likely that a few people within the company are going to be interested at the model you use, and what you plan to do with it. It is possible that these individuals are going to want to see the model and what you are doing long before you are actually ready to present it to them.

As you can imagine here, there is a dilemma. How are you meant to show to the other people in the company what you are doing, and how the model will work, in a manner that they will be able to understand, can be a challenge. And you may not have gotten very far in the work that you are doing yet, so how are you supposed to showcase all of the information yet?

Depending on the kind of problem that you are focusing on it is possible that you would have millions of different points of data to work with, and in the early stages of this model, it is easier to understand how you can be overwhelmed, but there are still steps that you can take in order to make everyone happy and showcase what you are going to do with a model, even to people who may not be able to understand all of the technical stuff, but still need to know what is going on with the information. But how is this all possible?

This is going to work with the Naïve Bayes algorithm, an algorithm that you are able to work with that ensures the programmer is able to stick with some of the earlier stages of the model, one that is easy to understand while you still show any and all of the information that you need at the time.

Let's take a look at how this is going to work with an example of apples. When you grab what is considered an average apple, you will easily be able to state that there are some distinguishing features that are present. This could include the fact that the apple is red, that it is round, and that it will be around three inches round. While these can sometimes be found in some other types of fruits, when all of these features are present together, then we know that the fruit in our hands is an apple. This is a basic way of thinking, but this is an example of working with the Naïve Bayes.

The Naïve Bayes model is meant to be easy for you to put together, and it is sometimes used to help you get through really large sets of data in a way that is simplified. One of the advantages of working with this model is that though it is simple, it is sometimes better to work with compared to the other, more sophisticated models that you can work with.

As you learn more about how to work with this algorithm, you will start to find that there are more and more reasons for you to work with it. This model is really easy to use, especially if you are a beginner to the world of deep learning and machine learning. You will also find that it can be really effective when it is time to make some predictions for our data sets and what class they should end up in. This makes it easier for you to keep things as simple as possible during the whole process. Even though the Naïve Bayes algorithm is really simple to work with, you will find that it is able to perform really well. In fact, when compared to some of the higher-class algorithms that are out there, and some of the ones that seem to be more sophisticated, this one is going to perform the best.

While we have spent some time talking about the different benefits that come with the Naïve Bayes algorithm, there are going to be some negatives that we need to watch out for as well. The first of these negatives is that when you work with this algorithm, one that is going to take on variables that are categorical, you have to make sure that any of the data you test hasn't already gone through a set of data to be trained. This algorithm is also going to struggle with some of the predictions it makes and how much accuracy is found there. The Naïve Bayes is going to rely mostly on probability rather than accuracy so keep this in mind as you go through and work on that data.

There are a few steps that you can take in order to help fight off this issue and to ensure that things are going to work out the way that you would like, it is sometimes confusing to know how to handle these steps and many beginners do not like to do this.

Of course, even with some of these negatives, the Naïve Bayes is going to be a good option to help out when you are doing some work with machine learning. But it is not going to have everything that you need each time that you start programming. For those coders who want to be able to take their information and get it set up in a simplified manner that is easy to read through and won't require you to add in a lot of complicated code, at least not yet, then the Naïve Bayes model is the right one for you.

Working with the regression algorithm

The second Python machine learning algorithm that we are going to focus on here is called the regression analysis. This algorithm is going to help you out when you would like to see whether there is any relationship, and what type of relationship, will show up between the two variables in your code, the predictor variable ad the dependent variable.

This is a technique that often works well when you would like to make sure you can check out whether there is a casual relationship that shows up in the forecasting part of the variable, or the time-series modeling in place. The reason that a programmer would want to work with the regression algorithm at all is that it is able to take ahold of the information that you have, and then can fit it back onto a simple curve, and often a line, as much as possible. There may be some points that are way far away from this line, but the line or the curve is set up to handle the majority of the data points as much as possible.

You will find that the regression algorithm is used by a variety of companies right now because it is so helpful for adding in any information that is needed and then sorting through it and seeing what is there. you can add in information about the current economy, or even the past economy for example, and then this algorithm is going to come up with an output as a prediction of how things will show up in the future. You have to make sure that the information you provide to the algorithm is up to date and accurate though, or this prediction is not going to be that accurate at all.

The thing that a lot of programmers are going to like about using the regression algorithm is that you can add in any kind of information that you need to it. You can add in information to help you know about some predictions on your profits to help you see any estimations it can come up with about the sales growth that may happen in your company. And it can even be used if the right information is added in to tell us more about the economy and how the market is doing now, and how it is likely to do in the future.

Let's take a look at how this can be done first. In this example, if you choose to work with the regression algorithm, and then you find out that the company is growing at a similar rate as what other industries are doing, or even other companies in the same industry, than you would be able to take this information and use it to make some good predictions on how you are likely to do in the future based on what decisions you are planning to make

As you look through the idea of regression algorithms, you will notice that there are more than one kind of regression algorithm that you are able to focus on based on what your end goal is all about and what information you would like the algorithm to show to you when it is all said and done. Some of the different types of regression algorithms that are available for you to try out as you do machine learning will include:

- Linear regression
- Polynomial regression
- Logistic regression
- Ridge regression
- Stepwise regression

As you can see, working with the regression algorithms are going to have a few different benefits that come with them. To start, you will see that these algorithms make it easy for anyone using the information to see what relationship is present, if any, between the dependent variables and the independent variables. This algorithm is also able to show what kind of impact will happen if you try to add in a new variable or change up another kind of variable that is in your data set.

Even though there are several benefits with this method, there are a few things to be away of when working on the regression algorithm. The biggest shortcoming that you will quickly notice is that you aren't able to use this algorithm to help out with any classification problem that comes up. The reason that classification problems and the regression algorithm don't always work together is because this particular algorithm tries to overfit the data many times. So, if you do try to add in different constraints here, you will find that the whole process is going to get tedious pretty quickly.

The clustering algorithms

We spent some time earlier looking at what are known as the clustering algorithms when we talked about the k-means clustering algorithm. But now we are going to dive a bit more into what these clustering algorithms are able to do, and why they are so important to learn all about when you do some machine learning.

When we are able to focus our attention on the clustering algorithms, we have to double check that these are kept simple, rather than adding in a lot of complexity. This method is meant to take on all of the data that you are working with, and then will create some clusters in order to put the points of data together before you start up an algorithm that relies on clustering, you will be able to benefit from choosing the number of clusters that you would like to work with. This is going to depend on how much data you are working with, and what you are planning on finding when the algorithm is done.

Let's say that you are working on a project where you would like to divide up your customers between male and females to start with. This kind of program would just need to have two clusters to sort people out. But if you would like to learn more about the different age groups of your customers, then dividing into five or six clusters could be a bit more useful. After you have been able to implement how many clusters you would like to work with, the program is able to add in the clusters and will make all of the data points fit into there

One of the things you will enjoy about this algorithm is that it is going to be able to take on most of the work that you need to do for you in the process. This is because it is going to take the information that you give about how many clusters you would like to use and then can add in all of the data points to the various clusters based on how they fit. This is going to ensure that the information is easy to read and is organized, and you will be surprised at the insights that you can gain from doing this kind of algorithm.

After the information has been sorted out into the various clusters it is possible that you will take a look at them and notice that there are a lot of different points that show up inside. It is safe to assume that the more points that fall inside a specific cluster, the more likely your target market fits in that group. Remember that the points that fit inside one cluster are going to be similar to one another, while not being similar to the points of data that show up in some of the other clusters that you have.

Once you have formed some of the original clusters, it is time for you to take an individual cluster and divide it up to get more sets of clusters, if this makes sense for what you want to get out of this algorithm. You are able to do this as many times as you want, creating a bunch of divisions as you go through each one. In fact, it is possible to go through these steps so many times that you will stop seeing changes as you do the work.

Now, there are going to be a lot of reasons why a programmer would want to work with these kinds of clustering algorithms when they do some work with machine learning. First, when you use a clustering algorithm to help with your computational work, it is much easier and more cost efficient to get the work done, especially when we look at some of the other options, the supervised learning options, that can do the same thing. And if you plan to work with some problems of classification, then these types of algorithms are the ones to get it all done.

With this in mind, it is important to remember that the clustering algorithm is not going to be the right one to work with every time that you do some machine learning. This algorithm is not going to show you predictions or tell you exactly what to do. You can look at the clusters and figure out some trends and make some decisions, but you have to be the one who does the work at coming up with the course of action.

What is the Markov algorithm?

Another type of unsupervised machine learning algorithm that you can work with is the Markov algorithm. This particular algorithm is going to take the data that you decide to input into it, and then it will translate it to help work in another coding language if you choose.

The nice thing here is that you can pick out which rules you want to use with this algorithm ahead of time so that the algorithm will work the way that you want. Many programmers in machine learning find that this algorithm, and the fact they can set up their own rules ahead of time, is nice because it allows you to take a string of data and ensure that it is as useful as possible as you learn on the job and figure out the parameters of how the data will behave.

Another thing that you may like about this Markov algorithm is that you are able to work with it in several ways, rather than being stuck with just one method. One option to consider here is that this algorithm works well with things like DNA. For example, you could take the DNA sequence of someone, and then use this algorithm to translate the information that is inside that sequence into some numerical values.

This can often make it easier for programmers, doctors, and scientists and more to know what information is present, and to make better predictions into the future. When you are working with programmer and computers, you will find that the numerical data is going to be much easier to sort through than other options of looking through DNA.

A good reason why you would need to use the Markov algorithm is because it is great at learning problems when you already know the input you want to use, but you are not sure about the parameters. This algorithm is going to be able to find insights that are inside of the information. In some cases these insights are hidden and this makes it hard for the other algorithms we have discussed to find them.

While there are a lot of benefits that can come with working on the Markov algorithm, it is important to know that this one can sometimes prove difficult for some beginners because they do have to go through it manually to create a new rule. This happens when they want to add in a new coding language to the work. If you only plan to work with Python while doing this, you only need to make the rules once and it is not that big of a deal. But if you do plan to work with several coding languages in machine learning at a time, then this could become a big hassle to work with.

Q-learning

We haven't had much of a chance to talk about any of the reinforcement types of machine learning that you are able to work with. This kind of machine learning is going to be a bit different than we would see with some of the other two types, in that it is going to rely mostly on true and false kind of learning rather than on teaching it with examples or letting it learn through the unsupervised machine learning method. This can make it easier for you to train the program how to react in the way that you would like, and can ensure that you are going to be able to see how different types of machine learning will work.

With that in mind, it is time to take a look at one of the algorithms that you can do with reinforcement learning known as Q-learning. With this kind of algorithm, you are going to find that it is the most effective, and it is going to work out the best, with something that is described as temporal difference learning.

Compared to a few of the other types of algorithms that we have talked about in this guidebook the Q-learning one would be considered an off-policy algorithm. This is because it is not going to have the abilities inside to learn an action value function. This may sound confusing, but it means that you are going to be able to get the results and the output, regardless of the kind of state you are in at the time.

Since you can take this Q-learning algorithm and use it no matter what function you are trying to create in machine learning, you will first need to take the time and go through your application and list out the specifications that you want to use. These specifications should tell us how the user, or even the learner, is going to select the action they want to take. This can take a bit more time and means you have more steps to do with the process, but it is definitely something that is worth the effort and the time.

After you have been able to go through and actually find all of the functions that are considered action value that you would like to use (read through them and see if they are actually useful for the code that you are writing, it is time for you to create your own optimal policy. One of the best methods that you need in order to construct this is to use the actions that you think would be seen as the highest value for your program, regardless of the kind of state that you would like to work in here.

Just like with any of the other algorithms that we have discussed in this guidebook, there are going to be a few benefits that come with using this algorithm. One of the benefits is that you won't have to worry about taking all of that time, or dealing with all of the effort, to put in the models of the environment in order to get the system to compare it. You can even go with the option of 6choosing to compare a couple different actions, and even many actions, at the same time.

As you can see, there are a lot of different types of algorithms that you are able to use when it comes to artificial intelligence and machine learning, and

Python, as well as a lot of the different libraries and extensions that come with it, are going to be able to help you get this done. Whether you want to work with supervised machine learning, unsupervised machine learning, or reinforcement learning, you are sure to find the results that match up with your chosen project, and what you would like to do.

This guidebook took some time to explore these different parts and to ensure that we know how to make them work. And with all of the options, we can really see how machine learning is going to take off and help us to grow and change technology like never before. Think about all of the cool things that are yet undiscovered, and that we have yet to do, when it comes to working with machine learning with Python.

Conclusion

Thank for making it through to the end of *Python Programming*, let's hope it was informative and able to provide you with all of the tools you need to achieve your goals whatever they may be.

The next step is to take a look at some of the different topics that we discussed in this guidebook. There is a lot of information to process through here and learn about when you want to do some of the various tasks, like machine learning and artificial intelligence, but you also want to be able to work with the ease and the power that comes with the Python coding language.

This guidebook took some time to explore a lot of the different topics that can come up with this. It is meant to help us understand how to work with Python, what is all available with Python, and so much more. And with all of the great libraries and other extensions and features that come with this language, it is no wonder that there are so many things that you are able to do with the help of

Python to make your own machine learning algorithms.

Working with machine learning is something that a lot of different companies want to focus on now. They like the idea of being able to get a system to learn while they are not there. they like to provide a better kind of customer service than they could before. And they like all of the doors and opportunities that are going to present themselves when it comes to this kind of programming. And when they can provide it all and learn how to do all of the different parts with the help of Python, that can just make that much easier.

Finally, if you found this book useful in any way, a review on Amazon is always appreciated!

Description

Have you been interested in expanding out your programming skills to include artificial intelligence and machine learning, but worry that it is going to be too hard? Have you worked in the Python language in the past and found that you enjoyed working with this coding language, but didn't think it could actually do something more advanced? Would you be interested in learning how to combine these two ideas together in order to make some powerful and strong codes in no time?

This guidebook is going to spend some time talking about Python programming, and how you can use it in order to work with such topics as artificial intelligence, machine learning, and deep learning all in one. We will explore how to download some of the various libraries that you need, how to set up some of the different learning algorithms that you need, and so much more.

Some of the different topics that we will discuss in this guidebook to help you to get started with coding in Python machine learning will include:

- What is deep learning and artificial intelligence
- What is machine learning and how it is taking us into the future.
- All about the Python coding language, and some of the best and most common libraries that can help us with machine learning.
- All the machine learning algorithms you need to know including Decision trees, linear classifier, Neural networks and more.

When you are ready to propel your coding into the future and learn more about machine learning, artificial intelligence, and the Python coding language, take a look at this guidebook and learn how to get started! Click on Buy Now to get started!

Copyright © 2019 by Marc Matthes

All rights reserved. **No part of this publication may be reproduced**, stored in a retrieval system or transmitted, in **any** form or by **any** means, electronic, mechanical, photocopying, recording or otherwise, without permission in writing from the publisher.

www.ingramcontent.com/pod-product-compliance
Lightning Source LLC
Chambersburg PA
CBHW070643220526
45466CB00001B/268